LIFE HACKS
FOR DADS

Handy Hints to Make Life Easier

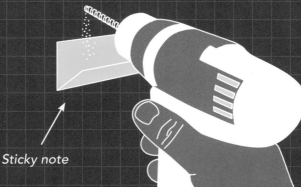

Sticky note

Cordless drill
(corded drills are
also acceptable)

summersdale

Dan Marshall

Over **100** amazing hacks inside!

DISCLAIMER

Neither the author nor the publisher can be held responsible
for any loss or claim arising out of the use, or misuse,
of the suggestions made herein.

CONTENTS

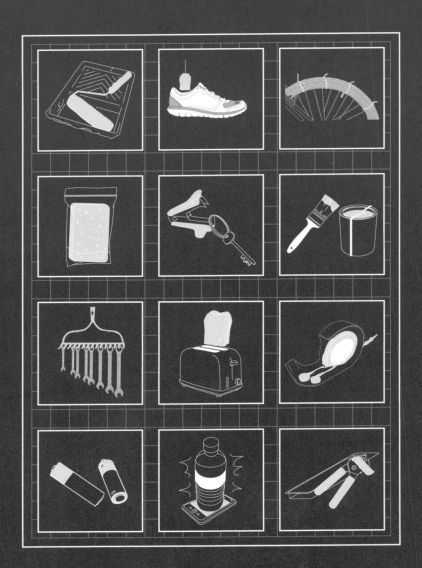

INTRODUCTION

Being a dad is tough. As a responsible parent, you're expected to dedicate time and attention to the upbringing of your child (or children) – essential things, like their ABCs. But where does that leave the three 'B's: beer, burgers and baseball? (Other sports work here too, but there are only so many beginning with 'b'.) The truth is, whatever you're into – be it books, board games or ballet – parental duties always require 'effort', and we here at the Life Hacks Institute are doing everything in our power to free mankind from this terrible, terrible burden.

Inside you'll find over a hundred ways to save time *and* effort: whether while cleaning up around the house, chowing down on some delicious takeaway, or helping little Johnny or Daisy have a kick-ass time with a cardboard box. In short, this book will help you in almost every aspect of your life (except maybe in the bedroom – if you made it to fatherhood, you're probably doing OK in that area already).

HOUSEHOLD HACKS

A dad's duties around the house can be challenging. Efficient snacking, for instance, is a serious business – and what's a guy to do when his novelty shirt collection has grown too large for the closet? Not to mention solving the age-old problem of keeping track of the TV remote. This chapter will help with all of these issues and more.

HEAVY-LIFTING HELPER

Having moved house several times, I must confess that this next hack never crossed my mind. I'm an idiot. An idiot with a bad back. Here's how it should be done.

If you're packing up to move house or simply storing the mountain of painfully expensive and now woefully neglected stack of toys that have been gathering dust for the past year, load heavy items into a suitcase with wheels and pull it to wherever it needs to go. The last thing you need is to load up a heavy box only to have the bottom fall out on you. Heavy things hurt when they land on your toes.

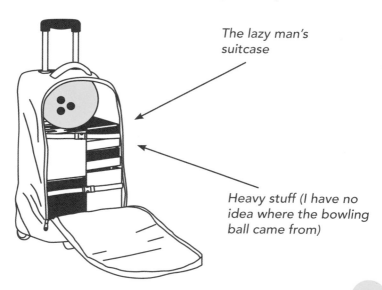

The lazy man's suitcase

Heavy stuff (I have no idea where the bowling ball came from)

WARDROBE EXPANSION KIT

Not having enough wardrobe space can be frustrating – maybe your closet has now become a library for your kids' finger-paintings? As a result, you're wondering where to hang your freshly laundered Rush T-shirts. Until now.

Save the ring pulls from cans of soft drinks and beer, and thread them onto the hook of a hanger, letting them rest at the bottom (where the hook meets the hanger itself). You have now created a loop to attach another hanger, thus doubling the capacity.

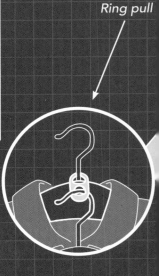

Ring pull

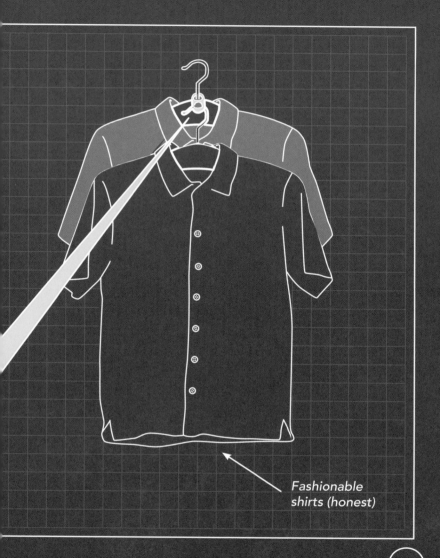

Fashionable
shirts (honest)

KEY-RING CRACKER

Sometime in the near future you might feel the need to add a tasteless novelty key ring to your bunch (or perhaps you got a *Dora the Explorer* key chain from your little darling last birthday?). Prising the key ring apart can be a pain.

To overcome this inconvenience, use a staple remover. Wedge the 'teeth' of the remover in-between the clasp of the ring, making it as easy as pie to slip on your new addition. Personally, I recommend a pewter Winnie the Pooh.

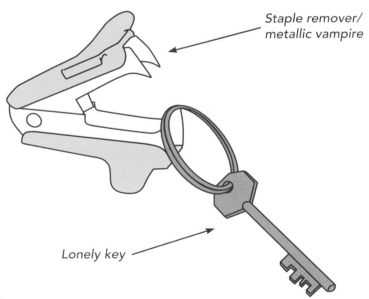

Staple remover/
metallic vampire

Lonely key

EASY-EMPTY RUBBISH BIN

If at home one of your many scintillating chores is to take out the trash, I feel your pain. When you have stuffed as much in there as humanly possible, trying to get the bag out can be tricky. This is due to the vacuum that is created when trying to yank the bin liner out. To rectify this little problem, get your power drill out (what do you mean you don't have one?!).

Drill a couple of holes at the bottom of the bin to stop the vacuum ever forming. The bin liner will now lift out with ease.

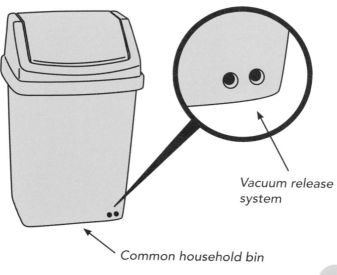

Vacuum release system

Common household bin

SMALL ITEM RETRIEVAL SYSTEM

Where do all those earring backs, contact lenses and Scuba Steve accessories go when you drop them? I'll tell you where: they're still there; it's just that you're too blind to see them.

When you drop something small and can't find it, grab your vacuum cleaner and a pair of old tights. Slip the tights over the vacuum nozzle and fix in place with an elastic band. Run the vacuum over the area where you think you dropped your item and, with a bit of luck, it will be sucked onto the tights, where you can pick it off with ease. If you find anything of value that isn't yours then remember this: finders keepers, losers weepers.

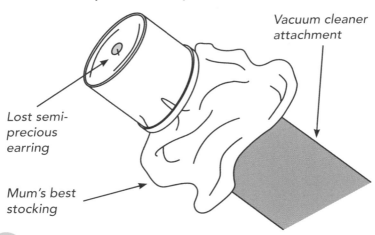

Vacuum cleaner attachment

Lost semi-precious earring

Mum's best stocking

VELCRO HOLDERS

Are you sick of losing the remote? I have to say that sometimes I find mine buried in the garden. If only there was a way of making sure that it stays put...

Velcro is your friend for this hack. Attach some to the back of the remote (use the kind with an adhesive backing, available at all good hardware stores) and its corresponding part to the edge of the coffee table, or wherever you want to keep the remote (not the bathroom). And you don't have to stop at the remote - go wild and figure out what else needs a more permanent home! (Note: using Velcro to strap your kids down in their seat will be frowned upon by the local authorities.)

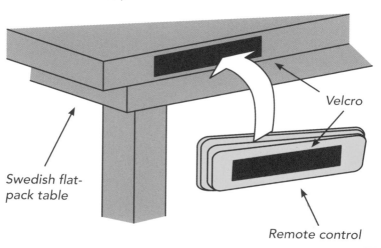

Velcro

Swedish flat-
pack table

Remote control

BATHROOM BUCKET FILL

When it's time to break out the mop and bucket in the bathroom, you'll have enough hassle getting into all those gross nooks and crannies – the last thing you want is extra effort lugging a scalding-hot bucket of water from the kitchen. Here's how to avoid that.

Place a bucket on the bathroom floor and put a dustpan in the sink (for this to work it has to be the type of dustpan where the brush can fit into the handle). Place the edge of the pan under the tap(s) and position the pan handle so it's jutting out over the edge of the sink. Now turn on the taps. The pretty waterfall it creates also doubles up as a very neat action figure waterslide.

Bucket (don't kick it!)

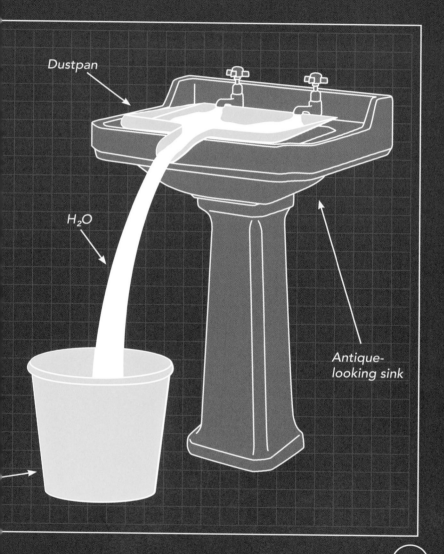

Dustpan

H_2O

Antique-looking sink

17

CRAYON REMOVER

Crayon scribbles on the wall are the bane of any household with young children. But this way of removing them (the scribbles, not the kids) will put your mind at ease.

Take a cloth, spray a little water-displacing lubricant on it (the kind that comes in a bold blue-and-yellow can) and apply to the offending area. The crayon marks will magically disappear!

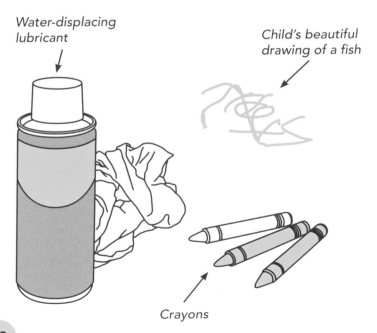

Water-displacing lubricant

Child's beautiful drawing of a fish

Crayons

HOODIE POPCORN HOLDER

Picture the scene: it's late at night and you've just settled down at your computer to do some serious Googling. Your beer is positioned within arm's reach, but wait... Where are the snacks? No problem. Put your hoodie on backwards, empty a bag of popcorn into the hood and voila – popcorn right in front of you. Just make sure the kids aren't around for this one – you've seen how piranha swarm a piece of meat...

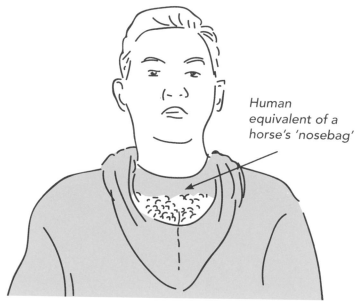

Human equivalent of a horse's 'nosebag'

DEAD BATTERY BOUNCE

If your kid's remote-controlled puppy is on the fritz, slamming it against the table won't help. Try this simple test instead: take out the batteries and drop them (negative side down) onto a hard surface to see if they bounce or not. A fresh alkaline battery will land with a thud and fall over when dropped from a height of an inch or two. A dead (or dying) battery will do a little bounce. Apparently, the 'good' battery contains a gel-like substance which absorbs any bounce, whereas the 'bad' battery has turned solid inside and recoils off a hard surface. So now you know.

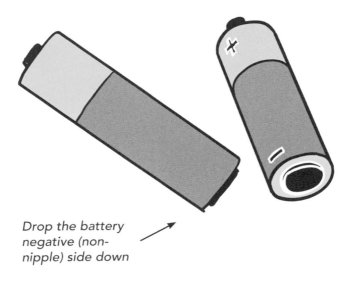

Drop the battery negative (non-nipple) side down

FOOD AND DRINK HACKS

Is there anything more important than food? Drink, perhaps – especially the cool, crisp, beery kind. Combine food and drink and you have what the French like to call a *raison d'être* and many dads call 'lunch'. The perfect beer/burger combo is something that has been coveted by generation after generation of fathers – the holy grail of meat-based barbeque foods and complementary beverages. It can be yours, too ...

PAPER BEER-CHILLER

Picture the scene: your buddies are coming over and you've forgotten to put the beer in the chiller: disaster! Don't worry. A simple paper-towel hack will save you from the wrath of those beer monsters.

Wet a paper towel, wrap it around your beer can/bottle and place it in the freezer for 15 minutes. When you take it out, the beer will be refreshingly crisp and cold for your guests – just remember to hide the imported beer before they arrive.

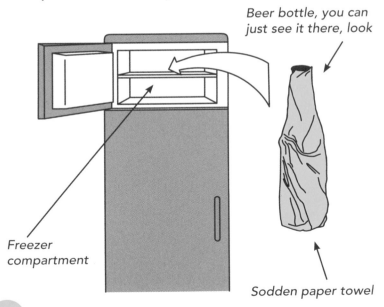

Beer bottle, you can just see it there, look

Freezer compartment

Sodden paper towel

SUPER-NUTCRACKER HANDS

Every dad wants to be seen as a superhero by their kids – chances are, you're not going to be able to achieve independent flight anytime soon, but here's something you can do. Prove your super-strength by cracking two walnuts with your bare hands. Place the nuts in your palm and line up the hard ridge of one of them with an indentation on the other – so they lock together, like a jigsaw. Close your hand around the nuts and apply firm pressure until they crack. Wrapping your other hand around the one holding the nuts to add additional pressure can help. But the one-handed nut crack is the mark of a true dad hero.

Super nutcracking energy is focussed here (awe on children's faces not pictured)

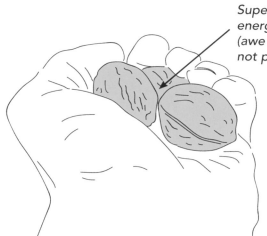

LEFTOVERS – PIZZA PARTY

Everybody hates tired old reheated pizza. The dough goes from crisp to chewy, and you end up gnashing and tearing away at the crust like you're gnawing on one of your kid's bouncy balls.

But worry not. There is a way to stop this unsightly way of eating. When reheating your pizza in the microwave, also place a glass containing some water in there and the crust will not dry out. Just try to eat it quietly, so you can have it all to yourself!

Microwave

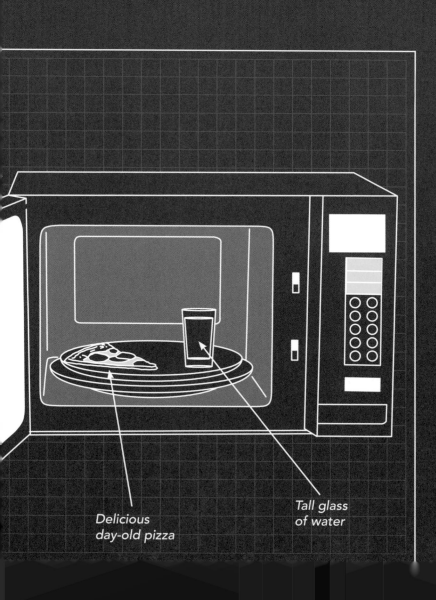

Delicious
day-old pizza

Tall glass
of water

INSTANT ICE-CREAM SUNDAE

The next time you've almost finished a jar of your favourite hazelnut or chocolate spread, don't feel sad... Now you can fill it with your favourite ice cream and create an instant ice-cream sundae! You can even add chopped fruit, whipped cream and those little sprinkles you put on your kids' cakes. If you're feeling generous, donate your delicious Life Hack treat to your little cherub – or hide in the basement and scoff the lot yourself. Your choice.

Sweet, sweet sundae topping

Delicious chocolate spread

BOOZY WATERMELON

Forget cocktails and punches: what you really need at any self-respecting soirée is oversized alcoholic fruit. This recipe is simplicity itself. Get yourself a watermelon and cut a hole in one side. Stick a bottle of vodka or rum in the hole (take the cap off first, dummy!) and leave it there until it drains completely. Alternatively, use a funnel and top it up with vodka periodically. Put the watermelon in the fridge to chill and, a day or two later, you'll have an impressive boozy treat to slice and serve to friends. Just make sure the kids don't try to nick a slice as one of their five-a-day!

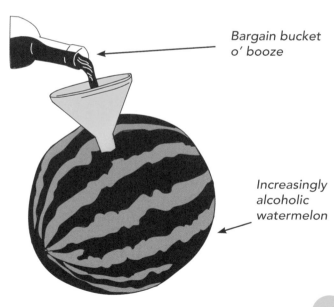

Bargain bucket o' booze

Increasingly alcoholic watermelon

LEFTOVERS – MICROWAVE MAGIC

How many times have you sat down in front of the TV with your conveniently microwaved leftovers, only to discover that somehow the food is cold in the middle, yet piping hot around the edge?

To avoid having to trudge back to the microwave to blast it again, try this hack out. Arrange the meal around the outside of the plate in a ring doughnut shape, leaving a hole in the middle. Now that there is no middle to stay cold, you will never again suffer a meal that is served at two vastly different temperatures.

Leftovers arranged in a pretty circle

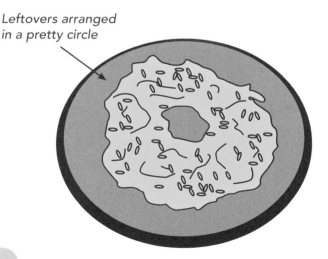

PAPER BOTTLE-OPENER

Desperate for a bottle of beer but can't find a bottle opener? Resorting to using your teeth or slamming the lid against something hard is not a good idea, unless you fancy a trip to the dentist or A&E. Instead, use this neat party trick: vertically fold a piece of A4 paper in half and keep folding it vertically until there's only a small amount of paper left. Then fold the paper lengthways to create a 'V' shape. Place this V against the underside of the lid of the bottle and, with one swift upward movement, you should be able to pop it open and release the imprisoned beer.

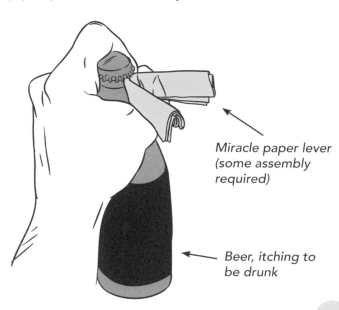

Miracle paper lever
(some assembly
required)

Beer, itching to
be drunk

THE ULTIMATE TOASTED SANDWICH

If, like me, your love for the perfectly toasted sandwich knows no bounds, read on.

When toasting the bread, place two pieces side-by-side into one slot of the toaster and slide the handle down. What do you get? That's right: a half-bread, half-toast hybrid! Add your favourite filling (mine's bacon with ketchup, if you're wondering), and tuck in. This is quite the sandwich, giving you the best of both worlds: crunchy toast on the outside and soft doughy bread on the inside. Dee-lish!

Slices of 'broast' →

Slices of bread

Toaster

CHEAP-WINE IMPROVER

If you've ever been sent out to the supermarket to pick up a 'nice' bottle of wine, only to be greeted by a look of utter dismay when you return with something that would be better used to degrease your engine, this one's for you.

Turn your bottle of Châteauneuf-du-Crap into something quaffable by running it through your blender for about 30 seconds (a hand-held blender should work too). This aerates the wine and allows the flavours to develop. It won't work magic, but it should improve the taste. Just wait for the froth to subside before you drink it – a wine moustache is not a good look.

Don't forget the lid, dufus

Aeration/Wine sploshing in action

JUICY ICE-CUBE BURGERS

The smell of burning wood and chargrilled meat (vegetarian options will be less meaty) is one of the greatest pleasures in a man's life – to provide your hungry pride with the spoils of the eight-burner grill is a proud moment. Before I break out into a sonnet about spare ribs, here's how to make sure your burgers are cooked to perfection: simply press a dimple into your raw burger patty with your thumb and place an ice cube into the space. As the meat cooks, the ice will melt and keep your burger moist and juicy.

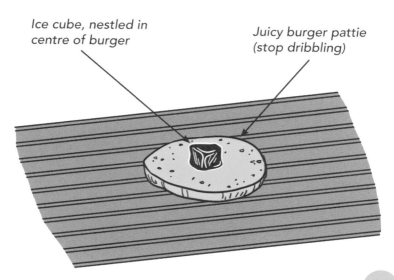

Ice cube, nestled in centre of burger

Juicy burger pattie (stop dribbling)

SIX-PACK DINING PACK

When dining al fresco (or, in my case, sitting on tiny chairs in a cramped garage), make it feel like you're eating out in a fancy restaurant garden – and save yourself trips back and forth to the kitchen – by using a makeshift cutlery caddy.

To create your caddy, simply save a cardboard six-pack holder (that's beer, for all you teetotallers). Put napkins, cutlery, salt and pepper shakers, and sauce bottles in the compartments, and there you have it: oh-so-classy dining at home.

Accompaniments

Utensils

The trusty six-pack

BEER

DIY HACKS

Doing it yourself is, for many dads, a staple. If you're not so hot with a power drill, you're cheating yourself – not least because nowadays it costs an arm and a leg to get some stranger in to fix what your grandad could have sorted out with a monkey wrench, some sticky tape and a lick of Brylcreem. On second thought, that may well have been the cause of, rather than the solution to, many of your household woes – so best get the hacks to fix that stuff yourself!

BLISTER PACK CRACK

Blister packs – the impenetrable rigid plastic packaging that all of your kids' toys come in nowadays – are the worst. Do these companies not want kids to play with their stuff or what?!

Even giant scissors can fail at this task. But there is a way. Take your blister pack and use a can opener along the side of it, thus opening the outer edge of the plastic monstrosity with comparative ease. Take that, evil blister pack inventor, you've been hacked!

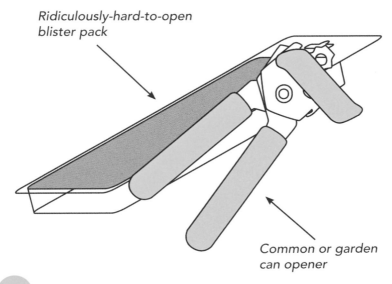

Ridiculously-hard-to-open blister pack

Common or garden can opener

NO-DUST DRILLING

The dust from drilling holes in walls can get everywhere (I've even found some on the cat). Here's how to make it mess-free.

When the drilling urge comes over you, grab your trusty power tool and a pack of sticky notes. Mark where you want to drill, stick a sticky note underneath and then fold it up to form a little trap for the dust. When you've finished drilling the hole, empty the dust in the bin and reattach the sticky note beneath the next drilling point. NB: this will not work with a hammer drill with a bit the size of your arm – that will need a whole pack of sticky notes.

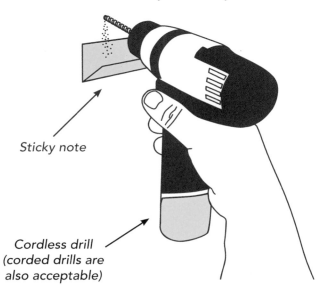

Sticky note

*Cordless drill
(corded drills are
also acceptable)*

ANTI-DRIP PAINT CAN

Fans of painting and decorating will like this one. Wiping the excess paint off your brush onto the side of the can might seem like a good idea at the time but will result in paint build-up, which is messy and makes the lid stick when you try to replace it.

To solve this, place an elastic band across the opening of the can. This creates a handy scraper for wiping the excess paint off your brush. When you have finished painting, simply remove the elastic band and fit the lid back on with ease.

Paint brush

Dirty elastic band,
dripping with paint

Immaculate
paint can

39

GARDEN RAKE TOOL ORGANISER

If your man-shed resembles a mini-junkyard, you're in for a treat (you have a man-shed, right?). No more hunting aimlessly for the right-sized wrench for the job, as this handy hack enables you to arrange your tools for ease of access. Take one old, rusty rake, detach the head and hang it up on the wall. Then organise your implements and stand back to admire your handiwork. This hack doubles as a stress-reliever. Tidy tools = tidy mind.

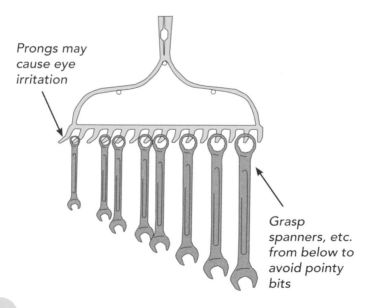

Prongs may cause eye irritation

Grasp spanners, etc. from below to avoid pointy bits

BREAD ERASER

Question: what do you do if your kids scribble all over your walls (and the hack on p.18 isn't suitable, because you don't want your living room to smell like an auto shop)? Get a slice of white bread (semi-stale works best), remove the crusts and scrunch the soft centre into a ball. Wipe the wall with a soft cloth and then rub your bread ball over the pencil or crayon to erase the offending marks. Yes, you could use an eraser, but scrubbing your walls with a carbohydrate is much more fun.

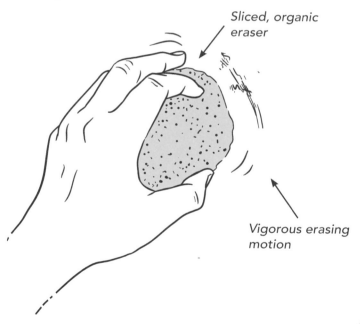

Sliced, organic eraser

Vigorous erasing motion

NON-SLIP RUG

You know how it is with kids – they wriggle, they run, they end up face-down on the floor crying their eyes out. No matter how much you supervise their playtime, falling over is a given, but you can do your best to avoid it.

If you have rugs and doormats that are devoid of a grippy underside, don't splash out on an expensive non-slip mat cut to size – simply apply some lines of acrylic sealant (the kind you use in the bathroom) to the bottom of the mat or rug and it should stay put. If you have to buy the sealant, you're now kitted out to reseal the bathtub and sink when the time comes – you're a regular DIY expert!

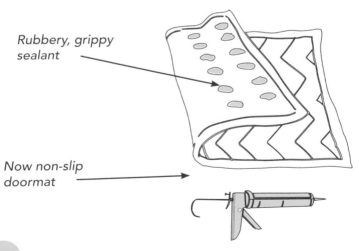

Rubbery, grippy sealant

Now non-slip doormat

POWER-CORD PERFECTION

Every guy has done it. You break out the lawn mower (or the vacuum cleaner) and instead of finding a power point nearer to the job, you go right ahead and plug it in a few feet from where you got it (maybe you're just unlucky and don't have a choice), meaning you have to stretch the full length of the cord to start work. So you're at risk of yanking the plug out of the wall while getting busy. Save yourself the humiliation of having to go back there and plug it in by installing a cleat near the socket – that way, you can wrap the power cord around an anchor point, making it impossible to unplug.

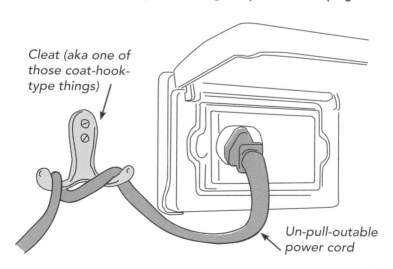

Cleat (aka one of those coat-hook-type things)

Un-pull-outable power cord

EASY-CLEAN PAINT TRAY

Paint trays are ruined after a few uses – old paint builds up and those useful ridges just disappear. Not good when little Daisy decides she doesn't like the fluorescent pink paint in her bedroom after all.

Here's how to keep your tray clean and functional. Line it with tinfoil before pouring in the paint. This will protect the tray itself and still allow the grooves to do their work. When you're done, simply remove the foil and throw it in the bin. Your paint tray will remain like new for years – unlike the walls, which will need a second coat or possibly a third. Better buy that jumbo roll of tinfoil.

Used paint tray
(still shiny)

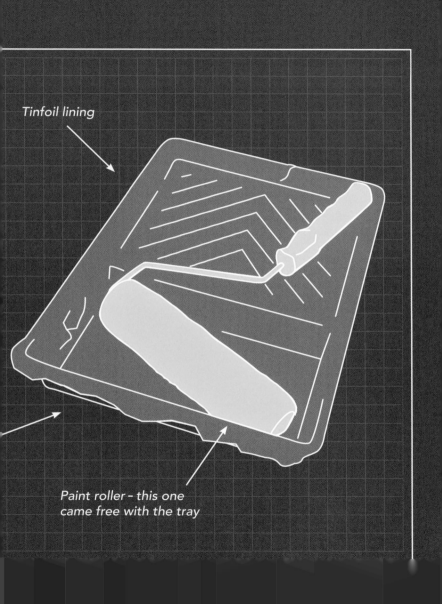

Tinfoil lining

Paint roller – this one
came free with the tray

RAZOR PAINT REMOVER

No matter how careful you are when painting, you will inevitably get some where it's not wanted. Like a carelessly discarded toy soldier, it can turn up ANYWHERE.

If you've been unlucky enough to inexplicably smear your best Armani tracksuit with paint, here's what you do: after the paint has dried, lay the suit on a flat surface and use a disposable razor to 'shave' the paint off the cloth in quick, short motions (don't press too hard, unless you're going for the cut-off look).

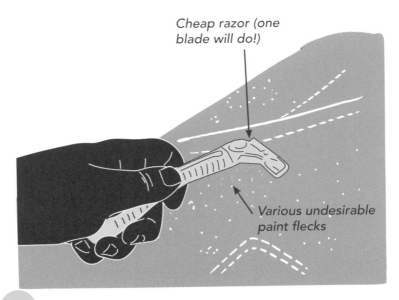

Cheap razor (one blade will do!)

Various undesirable paint flecks

COLA CLEAN-UP

An oil leak is bad news. Not only do they look unsightly, but the last thing you want is for your kids to slip on it or, worse yet, go poking their fingers into it and licking them afterwards. Clean it up safely and easily with this hack.

Simply empty out a couple of room-temperature cans of cola onto the stain (diet cola is optional, if you're watching your figure) and leave overnight. In the morning, dab the area with a few paper towels and you should have cleaned the worst of it off. Just don't let you kid see you pour on the cola, or they will definitely be licking it.

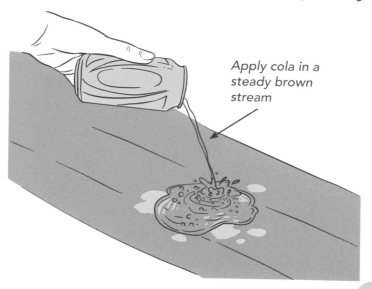

Apply cola in a steady brown stream

SCREWED SCREWS UNSCREWED

Who makes these screws with the heads that strip so easy? (No self-respecting dad should ever admit using too much force in this kind of situation – it was the screw, always the SCREW.) Well, anyway, there is a clever way to remedy the problem.

If your lame hardware has let you down yet again, grab yourself a rubber band and place it flat over the top of the screw head. Insert your screwdriver so it pins the band in place – now you have enough grip to get a proper purchase on the screw and finally get it out. Unless it breaks on you.

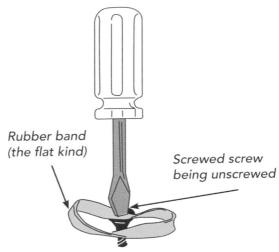

Rubber band
(the flat kind)

Screwed screw
being unscrewed

GADGET HACKS

Dads and gadgets go together like peanut butter and jelly – it's a sweet, sweet combo. Who wouldn't get excited about Airzookas, automatic tabletop twin disco balls and a golf glove that has a digital readout showing the pressure of your grip? Sane people, of course, but we're talking about needless technology here! However, if you're a fan of the concept but not of the price tag, the hacks in this chapter are for you.

RETRO PHONE STAND

Who said cassettes were dead? For a useful blast from the past, check this hack out.

Grab an old cassette tape case (no, not your mint-condition Hall and Oates album – use Cyndi Lauper instead). Fold the lid in on itself, towards the back side of the case, and rest it flat on your desk. Your obsolete piece of music packaging has now become a retro-chic smartphone holder, which will allow you to keep an eye of your incoming texts and emails while doing something more interesting or even to watch a movie on a tiny screen (I recommend *The Goonies*), just like home video in the 1980s.

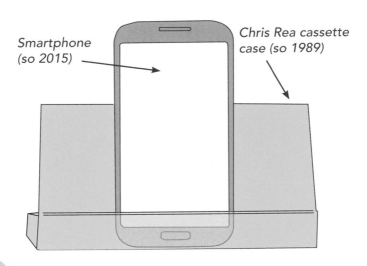

Smartphone
(so 2015)

Chris Rea cassette
case (so 1989)

CABLE ORGANISER

Wireless technology is a gift from the tech gods - but somehow, like hoverboards, it has yet to become ubiquitous. So, like so many dads out there, you probably have an entire drawer of cables. Time to sort them out.

Find yourself a sturdy box (the size should vary according to the amount of wires you have collected over the years) and begin collecting spent toilet paper rolls (enough to fill the box when standing them up vertically). When your collection is complete, fold your wires so that they fit snugly into the toilet rolls and place them in the box. You're on a roll!

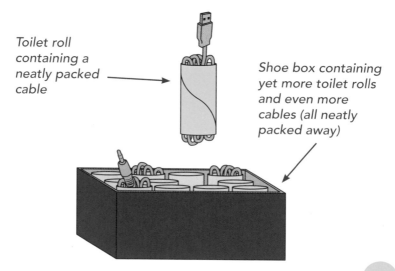

Toilet roll containing a neatly packed cable

Shoe box containing yet more toilet rolls and even more cables (all neatly packed away)

PHONE LANTERN

Dads and kids alike love shiny things. Here's one that could come in useful whether you're on a family camping trip or just bored one night while sitting out in the garden.

Putting a water bottle on top of your phone creates a makeshift lantern. The glow from the screen will turn the water bottle into a light so you can see in the dark whilst simultaneously attracting moths! Sure, it's more expensive and less useful than, say, your old-fashioned candle or torch, but where's the magic in that?

Water bottle

Moth-attracting light

Bright screen

LAPTOP COOLER

The beauty of gadgets is that they're at least 50 per cent unnecessary (I checked – it's the official standard). However, this can work against you when you're paying hard-earned cash for solid-gold crap.

Take, for instance, those fancy cooling pads to stop your laptop from overheating: 24 carat. I like to keep things nice and simple (i.e. free) by using an overturned empty egg carton. OK, it's not pretty, but it will ensure your computer gets lots of airflow where it needs it.

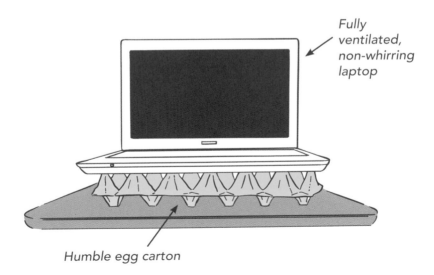

Fully ventilated, non-whirring laptop

Humble egg carton

BEANBAG CAMERA TRIPOD

If you're a fan of photography on a budget, you'll appreciate the awesomeness of a beanbag tripod. Yes, technically it has one wrinkly, squishy elephant-like leg instead of three – so if anything it's a uni-pod – but it's sturdy, simple to use and will cost you next to nothing to make.

Simply fill a cloth sack or bag with dried lentils or beans and sew the ends together or tie them shut. Plop it on the ground, or nestle it on a fence or rock, and say goodbye to shaky hands and blurry photos.

Fancy SLR (aren't you Mr Moneybags?!)

Mini beanbag from local tat shop (maybe not)

BONUS USB CHARGING POINT

Why do foreign countries insist on using oddly shaped plugs and sockets? This is especially frustrating when your child has been stuck on a plane for six hours and is desperate to watch the newest episode of *Blue's Clues* on your tablet. Well, no matter – here's a hack to help all you gadget-loving holidaymakers.

If you're abroad and have forgotten the plug adapters, it's handy to know that most TVs nowadays have a USB port in the back, which you can use to charge your electrical devices. Unless you've gone camping.

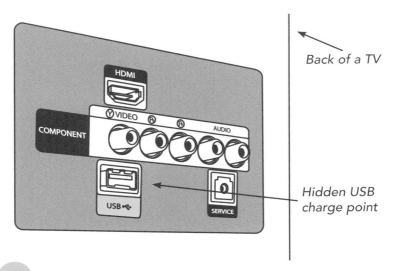

Back of a TV

Hidden USB charge point

COMPUTER TAB RESTORER

You know how it is: you're checking out the newest edition of *What Pizza?* online, your kid starts tugging on your trouser leg asking for a cookie, you get distracted and bam! You accidentally close down the tab containing all that must-have info.

Of course, you can't remember the exact web address and page you were viewing, so you have to trawl through your search history to find it. But not anymore! This simple keyboard shortcut will resurrect your discarded tab: Control + Shift + T (Command + Shift + T on a Mac). Memorise this little beauty – you'll wonder how you ever got by without it.

Digit-based keyboard pokers (aka fingers)

CHARGER HOLDALL

I love tripping over the mess created around the plug when my phone needs charging! Did the sarcasm show through there?

Keep your wires and phone out of the way with a clean plastic bottle. Remove the upper third of your chosen bottle (it should be big enough to house your phone and the charger wire) but keep the back of it intact. Next, cut a hole in the back that is big enough to allow your charger plug to fit through. You now have a hanging plastic pouch for your phone.

Power supply

Non-hazardous charging phone

Repurposed plastic bottle

IN-FLIGHT SMARTPHONE TV

If you're on a ten-hour flight to Tobago for the family hols and your plane doesn't have seat-back TVs, fret not. There's a simple solution that will keep you and your tribe happy. Put your phone in a clear plastic bag and attach it to the seat in front of you. Then sit back and relax. Your in-flight viewing system is ready for take-off!

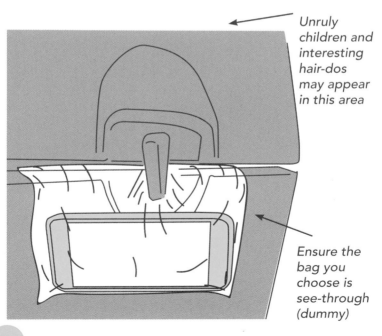

Unruly children and interesting hair-dos may appear in this area

Ensure the bag you choose is see-through (dummy)

EMERGENCY PHONE RESUSCITATOR

What you do in the comfort of your bathroom is your own damn business, but if you're like one in ten people and have dropped your smartphone into the crapper, you may want to take note of this one.

Speed is of the essence. Fish that sucker out of there and turn it off. Take out the SIM card, memory card and battery, and place them on a paper towel to dry. Wipe any moisture from your phone and then submerge it in a bag of uncooked rice. Leave your device for 72 hours so the rice can soak up any moisture. Then turn it on, hold your breath and see if it comes back to life. If it does, great. Now you just have to get over the fact that you're holding something that has been in your toilet up to your ear, mouth and face.

N.B. Do not attempt to eat the rice after this process

CHARGE BOOSTER

Just when you thought aeroplane mode couldn't get any more exciting, here's a hack that makes use of it. Turning on aeroplane mode while charging your phone will increase the speed at which the battery charges. This is especially useful for when you can sense a kid tantrum coming on - simply sit back, plug in the headphones and pretend you're asleep.

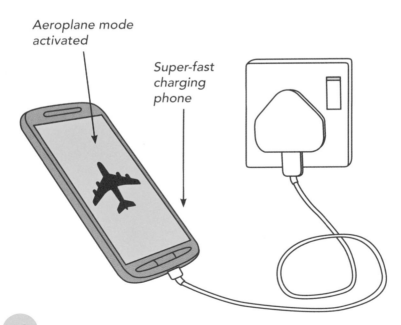

Aeroplane mode activated

Super-fast charging phone

HEALTH AND WELL-BEING HACKS

Staying in shape and in good health is important, especially if you're overusing the burger hack on p.33. But it can also be hard, expensive work – gym memberships cost more than car payments these days, and the bewildering array of health products at the pharmacy can be a nightmare (just how many different kinds of foot powder does the world need?!). Give yourself a break and approach things the Life Hacks way. Dads – you're worth it.

MOW YOURSELF SMARTER

You might not be in line to win the next Nobel prize for physics (if you are, then congratulations egghead), but there's no harm in wanting to improve your brainpower – at the very least, it's a good idea to hold on to what you've got upstairs. Especially when it's as easy as this.

Certain scientific studies have shown that simply mowing your lawn can release a stress-relieving chemical in the brain, and might even boost memory in older adults. So not only will you be keeping your garden in great shape, but you'll be weeding out the bad vibes in your brain too. All-round winner!

Unfortunately, no matter how smart you are, mowing the lawn will still be depressing

SMALL STOMACH, SMALLER PLATE

Are you looking to sculpt the ultimate 'dad bod'? Well, here's the solution.

Doughnuts! Just kidding. If you want to slim down and shed those unwanted pounds, you have to eat less. (Shock! horror!) To ensure this happens at mealtimes, put all your regular dinner plates in storage and break out the side plates (they're the smaller ones usually reserved for bread in posh restaurants). You'll find that you can't fit as much food on the plate, thus reducing your intake. Have a little discipline and don't go back for seconds!

To eat less use this one

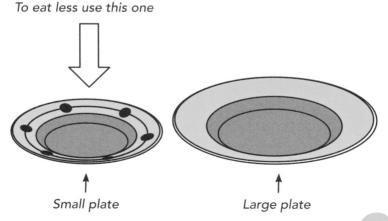

Small plate   *Large plate*

ASSISTED SPLINTER-REMOVAL

Dads are many things to their children –
one of them might well be 'boo-boo fixer'.
And arch enemy of the boo-boo fixer is:
The Splinter. Here's a way to make the
battle of good vs evil far less dramatic.

Pack a little baking soda into your travel
first-aid kit (don't tell me you haven't got
one!). When that splinter rears its ugly
head, wet the offending area with water
and sprinkle baking soda onto it, then
cover with a plaster.

Leave it for a day or so. When you peel
back the plaster the splinter will be raised
out of the skin, making it easy to pick out.

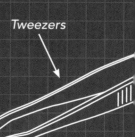

Tweezers

The offending splinter

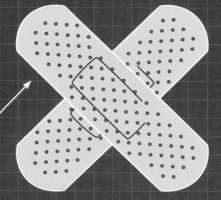

Baking soda

Plasters

WORKOUT PIGGY BANK

So you've decided to exercise a little more to get in shape, but those high-tech running shoes you shelled out for have been sitting in their box for the past six weeks. You need some monetary motivation.

Drop a coin into a tin or jar every time you hit the weights or go for a run, and by the end of the month, you'll look better, feel great and have a tidy sum to splurge on fancy fitness gear or something fun, like beer beetroot smoothies. Yes, in reality you are paying yourself to exercise, but you'll be amazed at how easily fooled you are.

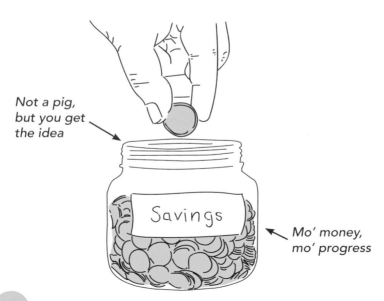

Not a pig, but you get the idea

Mo' money, mo' progress

SNUFF OUT YOUR SNIFFLES

Kids are germ magnets – they trade coughs and colds like rare Pokémon cards. And of course, they bring their bugs home for the whole family to enjoy. While there is still no cure for the common cold (surely somebody must be working on it?!), there are plenty of ways to combat it.

If you – or your kid – come down with the sniffles, you can fight back with horseradish. You may well be more likely to get your kid to eat a bar of soap, but if by some miracle you can get them to swallow a little spoonful (or at least take a good sniff from the jar) you could find that their breathing frees up. It's certainly a lot cheaper than your average cold remedy!

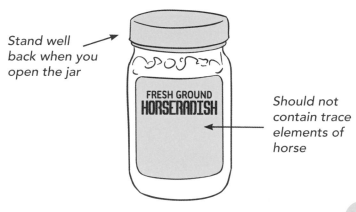

Stand well back when you open the jar

FRESH GROUND
HORSERADISH

Should not contain trace elements of horse

NON-DRIP ICE PACK

Sprained ankles and sore joints no longer have to be a soggy affair, but they will still be painful... sorry.

For a non-drip ice pack, soak a sponge in water and then put it into a ziplock bag before freezing it. When you come to use it, the melting ice will collect in the bag instead of running all over your nice clothes and carpet.

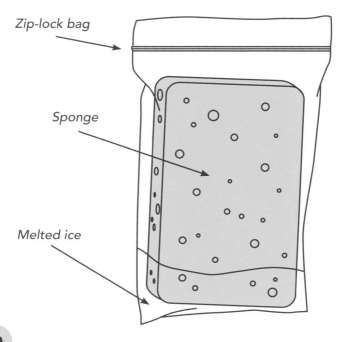

Zip-lock bag

Sponge

Melted ice

TICKLY THROAT RELIEVER

Ever had one of those infuriating itches in your throat that you just can't scratch? The next time this happens, try touching your ear. As crazy as it sounds, massaging your earlobe between your thumb and index finger will make the itch disappear. (No, it doesn't matter which earlobe you massage. Knock yourself out and massage both!) Massaging your ear stimulates nerves that can cause a tiny muscle in your throat to spasm, thus 'scratching' the maddening itch. If you're feeling lazy, make a game out of it and get your kid to do the hard work!

Work those lobes!

STOP SMOKING (SERIOUSLY, STOP IT)

It is a truth universally acknowledged that smoking is dumb. However, if you are unlucky enough to have started (and I can sympathise - I too wanted to look cool in front of the girls at school), here's something that's worth a try.

Although there's no substitute for professional medical advice from your doctor, you can give yourself a helping hand by visiting a sauna for three days in a row. The heat will help you to sweat out the toxins that have built up in your body, making it easier to quit.

Massive no-smoking sign just to drive the point home

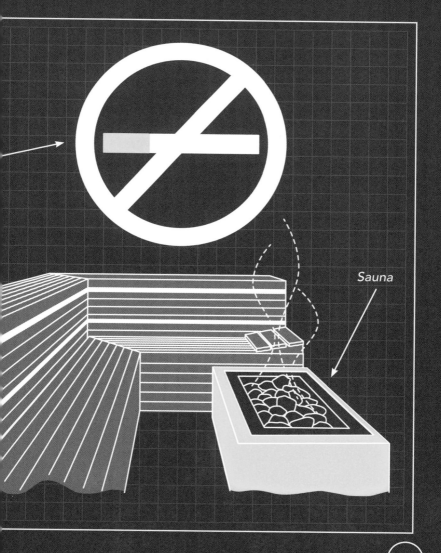

Sauna

73

CUSTOM HYDRATION SYSTEM

Well, technically, it's a cup... with lines on it. But this hack is quick and easy, and will yield lots of health benefits.

No doubt your doctor, your wife, your kids and the dog have at some point told you: 'Drink more water!' Sometimes it's the last thing you want to do, since it's so damn unexciting. However, something as simple as regular intake of water can help with concentration, digestion, energy – and just about everything else.

So get yourself a 1-litre drinks bottle and set out your intake, by time of day, on the side in marker pen. Now you have no excuse not to hydrate – even your cup is telling you to drink!

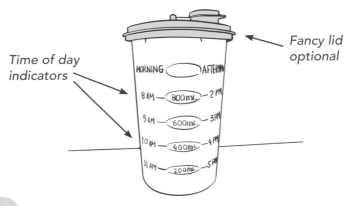

Fancy lid optional

Time of day indicators

MORNING   AFTERNOON

8 AM — 800mL — 2 PM

9 AM — 600mL — 3 PM

10 AM — 400mL — 4 PM

11 AM — 200mL — 5 PM

HACKS ON THE GO

Leaving the comfort of your armchair is something a dad just has to get used to. It's hard, especially when you've got your butt-groove moulded to perfection, but whether it's for business or pleasure, travelling will be on the cards at some point. This chapter is full of hacks to help you on your way.

MONKEY BANANA PEELER

Are you smarter than a monkey? Maybe you could give a chimp a run for his money on total body hair coverage, but chances are he will whoop you at peeling a banana.

Want to know why? Well, instead of grabbing the stem of the banana and wrenching it open, like most people do, chimps pinch the other (non-stem) end of the banana. This splits the skin in two, making it a cinch to peel. So, there you go: millions of years of evolution and we're only just realising we've been opening a banana upside down all our lives.

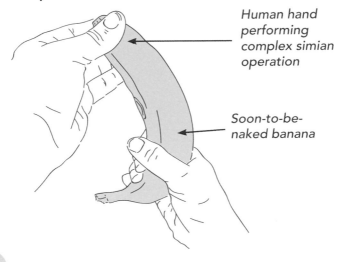

Human hand performing complex simian operation

Soon-to-be-naked banana

PRIVACY COAT HANGER

Staying in a hotel room where the curtains don't close all the way is a pain in the ass. Not only is there an unsightly gap which lets in light to disturb your precious sleep in the morning, but it will also prevent you from carelessly parading around in your shorts.

Here's how to hack your curtains. Raid the wardrobe and find one of those clothes hangers with clips for hanging up trousers. Turn it sideways onto the curtains and clip the ends of the curtains together. Gap removed; privacy restored.

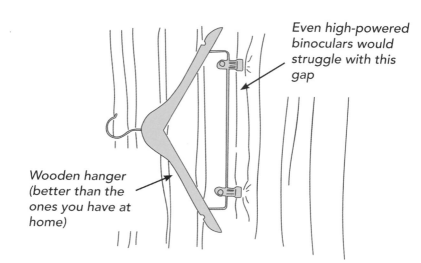

Even high-powered binoculars would struggle with this gap

Wooden hanger (better than the ones you have at home)

PORTABLE CRISP BOWLS

Snacks are a natural dad domain. A perfectly cooked and seasoned crisp is a minor culinary masterpiece, and an essential snack food at parties and picnics. Next time you have a get-together, impress your guests and kids alike with this hack.

Simply open your crisp packet and, slowly and carefully, scrunch up the bottom while pushing upwards: bam! You have yourself an instant snack bowl. Saves on lugging kitchenware around and requires no washing-up. Genius!

Sea salt and balsamic vinegar (too posh for the kids, you'll have to eat them yourself)

Nacho cheese
(eat before
the kids get a
chance)

THE BEER-MAT BEER SAVER

Unless you have an unnatural ability to empty your bladder without taking a pee, chances are that at some point while you're at a bar, you'll need to leave your drink and your seat. Fine if you're with friends – not cool if you're flying solo.

Here's a sure way to safeguard both. Simply place a beer mat or napkin over your drink – this lets any overzealous staff and would-be seat-stealers know that you've simply left the area temporarily. While you're up, grab yourself some nuts – you deserve it for being so smart.

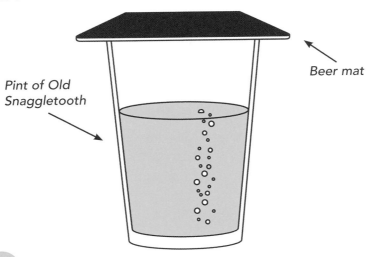

Beer mat

Pint of Old
Snaggletooth

KARABINER BAG-HOLDER

'What's a karabiner?' you ask. Well, for all you non-climbers, a karabiner is a roughly D-shaped metal ring that climbers attach their ropes to. You can pick them up fairly cheaply from outdoors stores and you'll need one for this hack!

When overladen with supermarket shopping bags, you can usually expect some kind of intense pain as the handles tear into the flesh on your fingers. Not anymore. Thread the handles of your bags onto your newly purchased karabiner and carry them all at once with no pain! Just don't use it for carrying your kids around; people will stare.

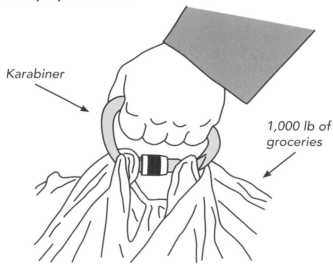

Karabiner

1,000 lb of groceries

MULTI-PURPOSE SHOWER CAP

Who knew there were so many uses for a hotel shower cap? I know you'd never be seen dead with one on your head, but this wondrous baggie can be used in a number of ingenious ways.

1) Cover your room service or takeaway leftovers with a shower cap to keep them fresh for longer.

2) Make the most of the hotel's breakfast buffet by taking an extra roll, boiled egg and ham, etc. and wrapping them in a shower cap ready for lunch!

3) Wrap your dirty shoes in a shower cap before packing your suitcase to keep your clothes squeaky clean.

4) Strap a toy figure to a shower cap and make a mini parachute to keep the kids entertained!

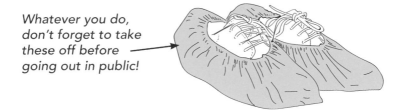

Whatever you do, don't forget to take these off before going out in public!

GET ON A ROLL

Whether you're going away for the weekend or jetting off to the Caribbean, smart packing will give you the edge – especially since airlines nowadays insist on reducing your luggage allowance to something Stuart Little would find portable. However, you can fight back with the 'Army Roll'.

You're bound to have plenty of T-shirts in your case, and it just so happens that they are supremely compactible. Lay your shirt out flat and make a cuff of about 4 cm at the bottom. Next, make two folds, left and right, to divide your shirt longways into thirds. Finally, take the collar end of your shirt and roll until you reach the cuff at the bottom – then tuck the roll into the cuff!

BALLOON EAR-POPPER

After a dip in the pool, do you ever experience a 'plugged' ear – when half the water in the pool seems to be stuck in your ear canal and all you can hear is muffled sounds? If so, this nifty trick should sort you out.

First of all, tilt your head to one side and gently tug on your earlobe. If that doesn't work, try blowing up a balloon. (What? You didn't pack balloons? What kind of a father are you?!) The pressure change should pop your clogged ears and hey presto, you can now hear your kids screaming and shouting again. Makes you want to jump back in the pool, doesn't it?

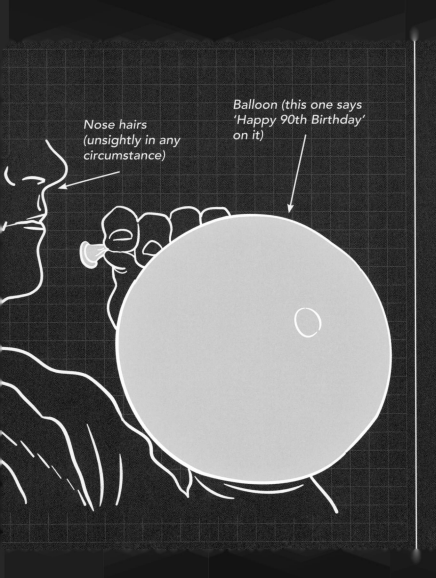

Nose hairs (unsightly in any circumstance)

Balloon (this one says 'Happy 90th Birthday' on it)

GLASS FLY REPELLENT

Whether you're on a picnic or eating outside at a restaurant, the last thing you want is to share your food with the indigenous insect population. Just how the hell does a fly the size of a peanut think it can finish a 24-oz T-bone anyway?

To deter those annoying buzzing critters, drop four or five pennies into a glass of water and place this on the table next to your food. The flies will think the pennies are giant, compound bug eyes and will steer clear – or at least move on to the next table.

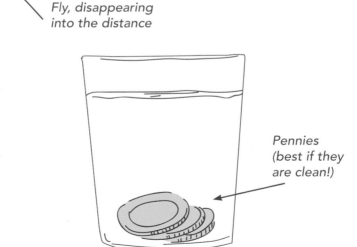

Fly, disappearing into the distance

Pennies (best if they are clean!)

CAR AND BIKE HACKS

Dads have been obsessing over the wheel and its practical applications for centuries. Modern man is blessed with power steering, parking sensors and cruise control, but half the time that's just something else that can break or go wrong. If you get around on two wheels rather than four, you have half a chance of fixing a problem yourself – but you never know when the next visit from the puncture fairy will be. So get wise and keep rolling with these car and bike hacks.

CAR REMOTE BOOSTER

What's the point of having a keyless entry system on your car if you have to be standing right by your vehicle to use the remote? Luckily, there's a simple way to extend its range.

If you hold your remote to your chin and open your mouth as you use it, the fluids in your head will act as an antenna and amplify the signal. Don't worry yourself with the science; just appreciate the fact that your head is a freakin' antenna! You're practically a Transformer.

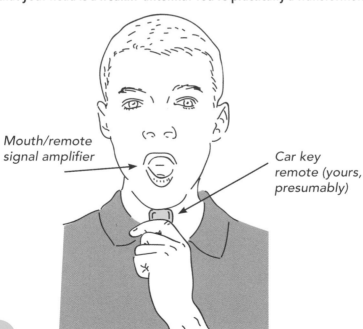

Mouth/remote signal amplifier

Car key remote (yours, presumably)

CAR DOOR BUMPER

Cars are expensive, especially when it comes to repairs. So, to save your hard-earned cash for more important things, why not reduce the likelihood of car damage?

Cut a pool noodle in half and stick it to the wall of your garage; that way, if you are a bit overzealous when opening the door once you've parked, you will prevent it from looking like it's been chewed by Jaws from James Bond.

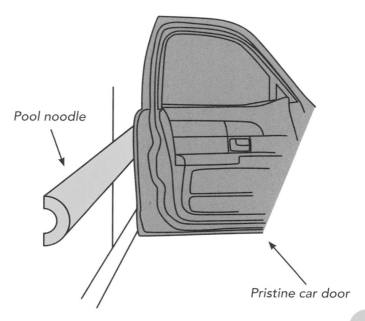

Pool noodle

Pristine car door

IN-CAR HOSTESS TROLLEY

This hack is for pizza-loving dads who can afford luxury extras in their car. If, like me, you live out in the sticks, takeaway delivery isn't an option. How are you going to transport your pizza/burger/curry without it getting cold by the time you get home?

Here's how. Turn on the passenger-side seat warmer during the drive up to the takeaway place (move all passengers to the back seat, obviously) and place your food on the seat for the drive home. When you finally get back, your delicious meal will be piping hot. Let's just hope they haven't forgotten the extra jalapeños!

Button for seat heater

Piping hot pizza

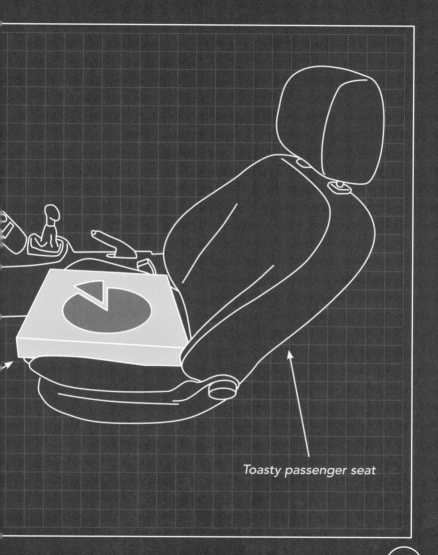

Toasty passenger seat

CAR CRASH SAFETY SPLASH

OK, so this scenario is a touch unlikely, but it's better to be safe than sorry! A madman is driving straight at you with the intention of mowing you down. What do you do?

To avoid going under the car, where you will sustain life-threatening injuries, jump up before the other vehicle hits you. You will hopefully roll over the top of the car and your injuries will be less severe. If you're a little more athletic, you could try jumping over the car. I've seen it done but, admittedly, it was in a kung-fu movie.

Unlucky/lucky RTA victim, depending on how high they can jump

Speeding vehicle of a driver under the influence

HEADLIGHT BRIGHTENER

Fogged-up headlights on a car you're trying to sell are a nightmare – they look bad and show the car's age. (With my clapped-out piece of crap, this is the least of my worries, but I like to make improvements where I can.)

To have those headlights looking like new, grab yourself some toothpaste. Yes, that's right: toothpaste. Scrub the headlights with a small amount, rinse and watch them sparkle. Just make sure you don't use your kid's toothbrush.

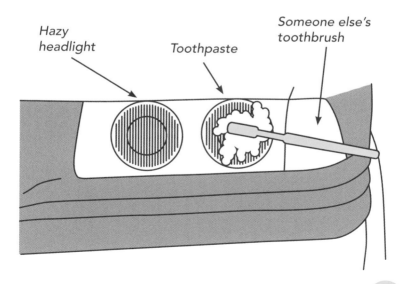

Hazy headlight

Toothpaste

Someone else's toothbrush

CAR FENG SHUI

This hack is so simple you'll wonder how you never thought of it before. During the winter months, when snow and ice are a problem, park your car at night so that it faces east. As the sun rises in the morning, the car will receive a burst of healing energy and… well, no, not really. It will help to defrost your windscreen, though, and save you having to mess around for hours in sub-zero temperatures with a scraper.

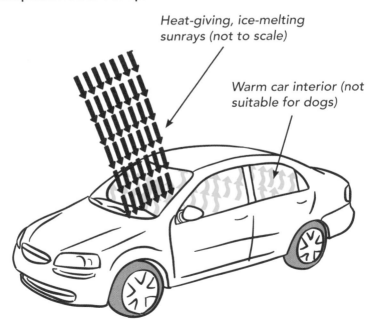

Heat-giving, ice-melting sunrays (not to scale)

Warm car interior (not suitable for dogs)

PETROL CAP PREDICTOR

So you've picked up your brand-new car/jeep/truck and you're determined to take it for a spin before you head home. You're high on new-car smell and suddenly you've killed a whole afternoon – and now you need to fill up the tank. But in all the excitement you forgot to check which side the gas cap is on.

Don't sweat it. Look at the fuel icon on the car's dashboard. If there's an arrow pointing to the left or right, this indicates where the fuel cap is. Sadly, older vehicles don't use this secret code, so if you're driving a car with no arrowhead on the petrol pump graphic, you'll have to resort to an age-old method: get out the car and take a look.

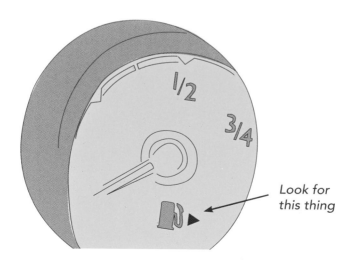

Look for this thing

BUDGET BIKE RACK

It's easy to get overexcited in the world of cycling accessories. There's a product for just about everything, and you'd better believe they're expensive. But you don't have to fall for it – especially when it comes to bike storage. This hack is simple, presuming you have enough space to store your bike vertically and adjacent to the wall rather than flat against it.

A certain Swedish homeware store is known for selling cheap brackets that make a remarkably good holder for your bike. The brackets in question are supposed to steady a track rail, but if you turn them the other way up, you get a simple pair of handlebar hooks. As long as you place them correctly, you've got yourself a budget bike rack.

Expensive, super-hi-tech bike

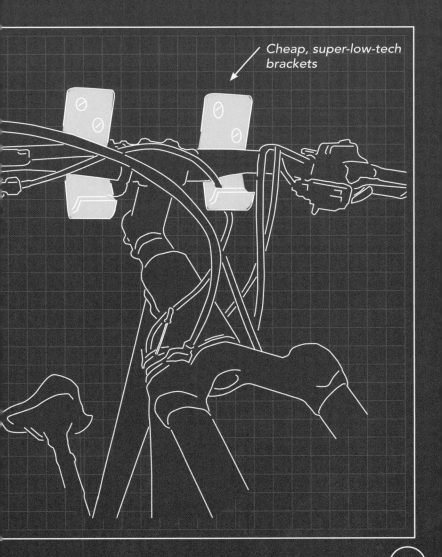

Cheap, super-low-tech brackets

DE-STINK YOUR WATER BOTTLE

Even if you buy the special kind of water bottle that has no synthetics whatever added, eventually it's going to get funky – and we're not talking James Brown here. Even if you put nothing in it but water, bacteria can still multiply, especially round the mouthpiece. Here's how to de-stink your water bottle without resorting to nasty chemicals.

Add two to three teaspoons of baking soda to your bottle and fill it with warm water. Leave it to soak for a few hours, then wash and rinse thoroughly. Perform the sniff test. If there's still a funk, try using denture tablets instead (downside: they're less natural and it's hard not to think about their intended use).

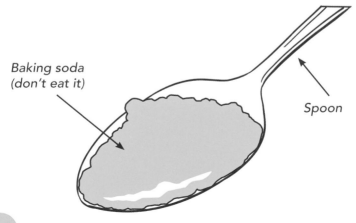

Baking soda (don't eat it)

Spoon

DIY SNOW TYRES

This one is for you hard-core, all-weather, I-don't-care-if-it-looks-like-a-winter-wonderland-out-there cyclists. Aside from seeking advice from a local mental health professional in order to regain your sense of reason, here's how you can tackle the snow more effectively on your bike.

If you must ride in the snow, make sure you have some zip ties ready. Fasten them one by one at intervals around your wheel, so they wrap around your tyre and rim, with the fastener part tyre-side out. Trim off the excess on each tie and you have yourself a set of makeshift snow tyres, which will work in a similar way to chains on your car wheels.

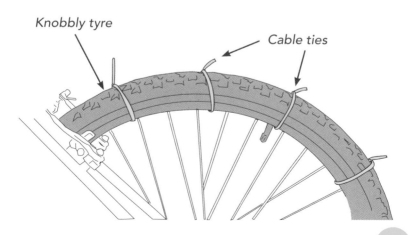

Knobbly tyre

Cable ties

SUGAR HAND DEGREASER

Working on your bike (or your car, for that matter) can be dirty – even if you use those weird airport-security, cavity-inspection gloves. If you can afford fancy degreaser handwash, all power to you – but if that's a luxury you can't afford then here's how to clean up the Life Hacks way.

Take a teaspoon of granulated sugar in your hand and add a splash of water. Scrub your hands with the sweet paste and wash them as normal, with a little dish soap for extra cleaning power. And there you have it: hands you could eat your dinner off. Well, maybe not.

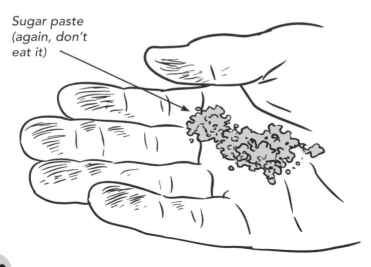

Sugar paste
(again, don't
eat it)

HACKS FOR THE KIDS

Caring for your children is what makes a good dad (at least that's what they said last time I saw *The Jerry Springer Show*), so mastering the art is essential. Yes, it can be hard – but it can also be fun, and it's the perfect excuse to act like a big kid (some more). Just don't blame me if you get a bruised butt because you couldn't resist trying out the stairway slide. Use these hacks wisely and safely.

MAGIC BANANA MESSAGES

We've already covered how best to peel a banana (see p.76) – and just when you thought things couldn't get any cooler...

That weirdly shaped yellow fruit actually has the power to convey secret messages. So, presuming your kid doesn't hate bananas, here's a hack to brighten their day. Grab a toothpick or something sharp, and scratch a message onto the skin of the banana. It won't look like much at first but give it an hour or two and the peel will turn brown, revealing your message as if by magic! Perfect for kids' lunch boxes. (Also good for pranking co-workers.)

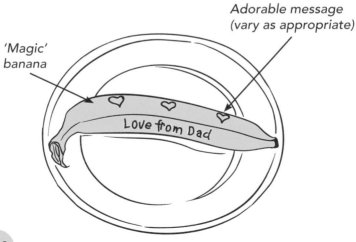

Adorable message
(vary as appropriate)

'Magic' banana

Love from Dad

MESS-FREE PAINTING

This next hack is great for when you want to do some painting with your kid but can't face clearing up afterwards. Let's be honest: kids + paint = domestic Armageddon.

Squirt some paint into a sealable bag (the large kind you use for freezing food) and tape the bag to a window, making sure it's well sealed. Your child can then create a masterpiece with their hands, and you can put your feet up and admire their handiwork. This hack is fun, educational, creative *and* mess-free! What's not to love?

Modern art masterpiece

Sealable freezer bag (God help you if it isn't sealed)

BEDTIME BUMPER

This hack will prevent many a bump in the night for anxious parents whose kids seem to involuntarily fall out of bed, having been transferred from their sturdy, enclosed four-sided cot.

Get hold of a pool noodle and place it under a fitted sheet on the side of the mattress open to the room, creating a soft barrier. The noodle will prevent your beloved child from rolling over and out of the bed in the middle of the night, saving injury and adding bonus hours of sleep to your already-starved routine.

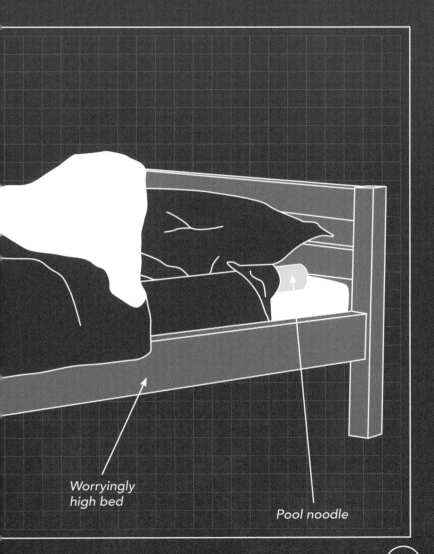

Worryingly
high bed

Pool noodle

BUG-PROOF DRINK COVER

Nobody likes bugs in their beverage and kids are no exception. Luckily, there's a simple solution.

During a birthday party or picnic you can protect your child's juice from thirsty bugs by cutting a small X into the centre of a cupcake case and poking a straw through. Voila! A bug-proof drink cover! Your kids will get a super-cute drink and you can relax, safe in the knowledge that the bees and bugs will realise they're not invited to the festivities and buzz off elsewhere.

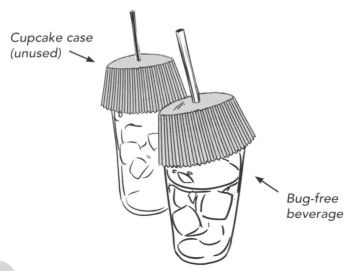

*Cupcake case
(unused)*

*Bug-free
beverage*

INSTANT TABLE HAMMOCK

Next time you want your little one to take a nap but he or she isn't playing, try this clever hack.

Tie a large bedsheet around the top of a table to create a fun mini hammock they'll be itching to climb into. Just a few health and safety notes: test your construction for safety and don't tie the hammock too high off the ground. A bedsheet can only hold so much weight so this is best for small kids only. (And do not, I repeat, DO NOT climb in there yourself!)

That bedsheet you never liked

Blissfully happy child

ICE CUBE TRAY SNACK CADDY

Do your kids look at a lovingly prepared plate of fruit and vegetables as if you've just put a pile of hairy cat poop in front of them? If so, this hack could be the answer to your prayers.

Try placing a variety of different bite-sized morsels in an ice cube tray and make choosing which piece to eat a game. This magically makes healthy snacks more appealing and it's perfect for the pernickety child who likes to keep their snacks separate.

'Groovy' grapes

'Brilliant' blueberries

Probably best not to eat that

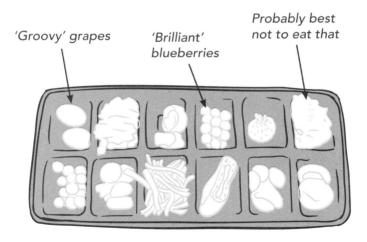

THE FRISBEE THROW

We've all seen college kids parading about on the beach or at the park with a Frisbee, looking cool. But they can never throw the Frisbee quite right, can they? Here's your chance to beat them at their own game and be a role model for your kid at the same time.

Get your perfectly un-toned backside up off the sand and intercept that Frisbee. Or you could simply ask to join in – that would work too. To throw a Frisbee correctly remember to use the same action as you would when you whip a towel (come on, we've all done it!). The Frisbee will now fly as straight as an arrow. Congratulations, you are now part of their elite club.

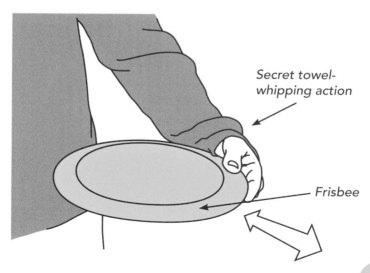

Secret towel-whipping action

Frisbee

DIY STAIRWAY SLIDE

A houseful of bored kids cooped up at home is every dad's worst nightmare. This hack will keep them entertained for hours and turn you into the coolest parent alive.

Remember that cardboard box your rowing machine came in (yes, the one that's gathering dust in the spare bedroom)? You can use it to build an awesome stair slide. Here's how: flatten the box and tape the cardboard to the stair wall using masking tape. Pile pillows and blankets at the bottom to make a soft landing pad and then let the super-happy, fun-sliding times begin! Just remember to give the kids a turn.

Shock-proofed child

Thick, snag-free cardboard slope

Arrows indicate recommended direction for use

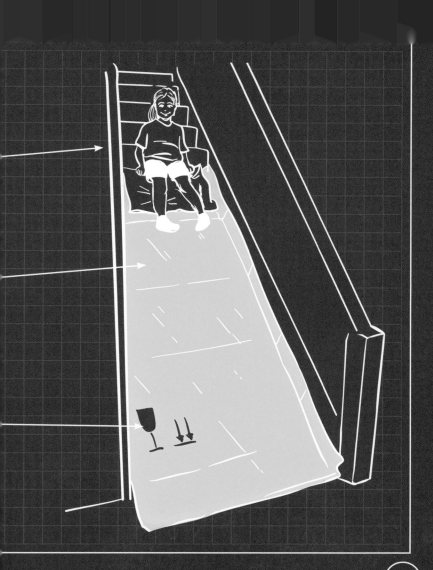

ICE LOLLY DRIP-CATCHERS

Remember those cupcake cases you used to stop bugs bathing in your kid's drink? (see p.106). Well, break 'em out again!

This time you're going to use them to catch the drips from your kid's delicious ice lolly. Simply poke the lolly stick down through the middle of an upturned cake case to create a little cup that will catch the offending drips. Now, if only there was a hack to combat brain freeze…

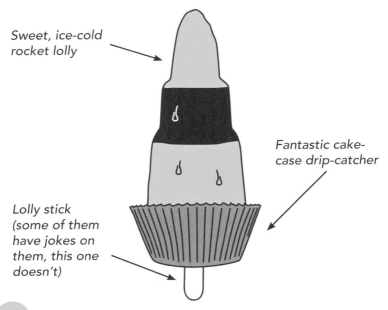

Sweet, ice-cold rocket lolly

Fantastic cake-case drip-catcher

Lolly stick (some of them have jokes on them, this one doesn't)

APPLE SLICE TRICK

It's amazing how much better an apple tastes to a kid when it's sliced! Here's how to utilise this fact to ensure that your children eat their five-a-day.

Slice an apple into segments and secure the slices together with a rubber band. This will stop them from turning brown. (No one likes brown apples.) Toss this into your kid's lunchbox or take it with you when you're out and about. Whip off the rubber band and you'll have fresh apple slices to hand. Works well for big kids, too.

Ready-sliced apple

Rubber band (not edible)

GLOW-IN-THE-DARK BOWLING

It might be inconceivable to some, but the game of tenpin bowling can be made better (in fact, this pretty much goes for anything): make it GLOW IN THE DARK!

Here's what you'll need: six glow sticks, six plastic water bottles (labels removed) full of water, a ball heavy enough to knock down your bottles (a basketball or football usually does the trick), and a pen and paper to keep score.

Pour a little water out of each bottle and pop a glow stick inside each one. Set up your 'bowling pins' in a triangle formation and take it in turns to try to knock them down with your ball. Unlike going to a commercial bowling alley, this activity won't require you to take out a second mortgage on your house, and you get to wear your own shoes!

Water-filled bottles

Glowsticks

GARDEN AND OUTDOOR HACKS

If you're lucky enough to have a backyard with grass and trees for your kids to enjoy, you're going to have to put some effort into keeping it clean and tidy – no matter how many burners your BBQ has, if your garden is full of weeds, your friends will notice. And if you want your kid to be the next Bear Grylls, you need to brave the wild outdoors (drinking your own pee is optional).

SAND STORAGE FOR TOOLS

There are three good reasons to keep a bucket of sand in your garden: 1) you can sit in your deckchair sipping a margarita, pretending you're on holiday in the Bahamas, 2) your kid can use it to play in and 3) you can store your garden tools in the sand to stop them from rusting.

Simply fill a container with builder's sand (note: avoid a trip to the beach, as salt and metal don't mix) and 'plant' your garden tools in it, with the handles sticking up. The sand will protect against rust and corrosion; also, as sand is abrasive, it will help to keep your tools clean and sharp – you dig?

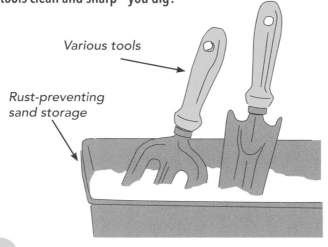

Various tools

Rust-preventing sand storage

BAKING SODA WEEDKILLER

For those of us who covet a pristine patio or driveway, weeds are the stuff of nightmares. And if you have them bad, you'll stop at nothing short of detonating a nuclear warhead to make sure they don't come back.

But there is a less apocalyptic way to free your driveway: pour a thick layer of baking soda into the cracks where the weeds rear their ugly head. Sodium has the effect of drying out plant foliage, which means those dastardly dandelions will be a thing of the past.

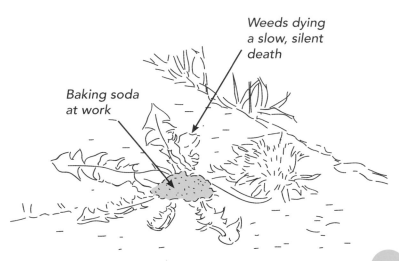

Weeds dying a slow, silent death

Baking soda at work

GARDEN HOSE REPAIR

Rubber hose has got to be up at the top of the list of least exciting things to spend your hard-earned cash on. What makes matters worse is that something that is basically a piece of rubber tubing costs the earth! So when your hose springs a leak – because the dog mistook it for its tail or your kid decided to use it as a swing – don't panic.

Simply locate those toothpicks you bought a few years ago (they're usually at the back of the kitchen cupboard, along with the cocktail recipe book from 1985). Then find the hole, jam a toothpick into it and snap it off. This will plug the leak, at least long enough for you to get used to the idea that you need to buy a new one.

Water-logged lawn

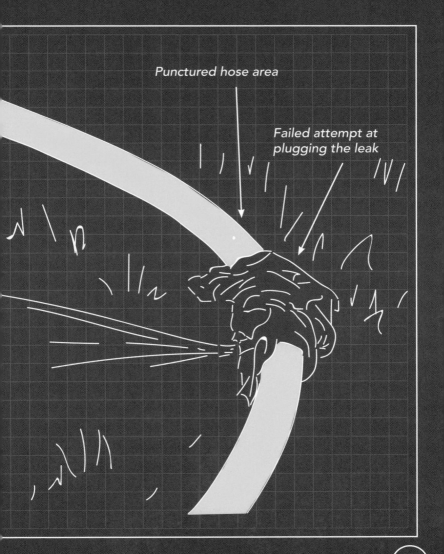

TWO-FOR-ONE HERBS

Supermarket herbs are not designed to last – that's why they keel over the second you walk through your front door. Instead of giving the supermarkets more of your hard-earned money, try this: split your potted herb into two and plant in good potting compost in individual containers. Most herbs die early because there are too many plants crammed into one pot. Give them space to breathe and you should prolong their lifespan and get double the herbs for your money. Even better, grow your own herbs from seed (I'll have to stick to supermarket ones; our family's 'green finger' skipped a generation with me).

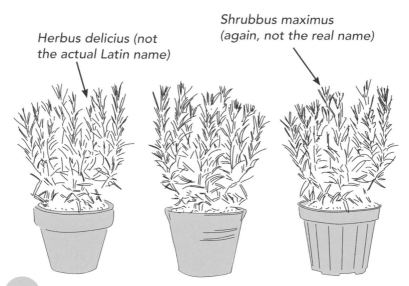

Herbus delicius (not the actual Latin name)

Shrubbus maximus (again, not the real name)

POTATO RUST-REMOVER

If you've noticed that your tools or your garden furniture have started to rust, ignoring it won't make it go away (trust me, I've tried). In fact, the longer you leave it, the worse it will get.

So it's time to man up with potato power! Yeah, that's right. This mighty vegetable contains oxalic acid which dissolves rust, so cut a raw potato in half and use it to scrub the offending area clean. For extra umph, dip the surface of the potato in baking soda or salt. This will make your veggie rust-remover more abrasive. Just don't expect to make French fries with the leftovers.

Rust-busting ingredients are hidden inside

COFFEE CRITTER REPELLENT

Slugs and snails are all well and good when your kids are putting them in their mouths, but they don't play well with plants. If you're trying to win the prize for most irregularly shaped turnip at this year's county fair, you might want to give this a try.

Take the leftover grounds from your morning cup of Joe and sprinkle them around your plants. Not only will this enrich your soil with nitrogen, but it will also repel unwanted guests such as slugs, snails and ants (apparently, they hate the smell and texture of coffee grounds). You hate coffee too? No problem. Stop by your local coffee shop and ask for some spent coffee grounds – they have mountains of the stuff to get rid of and should be more than happy to unload some of their garbage.

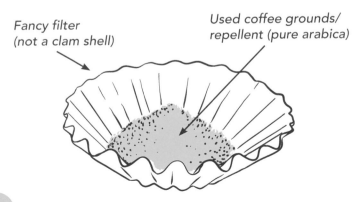

Fancy filter (not a clam shell)

Used coffee grounds/ repellent (pure arabica)

DAYLIGHT MEASURE

Here's a hack for when you're having fun in the great outdoors. Imagine you and your family are out walking – it's getting late and you're worried that you might not make it back to camp before dark. Put your mind at ease (or not) by estimating the amount of daylight left using nothing other than your bare hand.

Hold your arm parallel to the horizon with your fingers straight and your thumb tucked in. Line your index finger with the bottom of the sun and count how many finger-widths there are between the sun and the horizon. Each finger equals roughly 15 minutes of daylight. If there are five minutes of daylight left, pick up the kids and your wife, and start running!

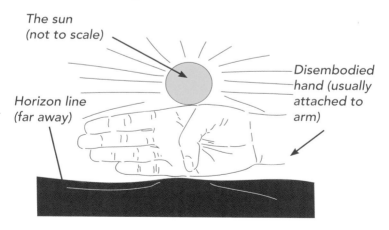

The sun (not to scale)

Disembodied hand (usually attached to arm)

Horizon line (far away)

BUG-BITE RELIEVER

Everybody loves the summer sun – fewer people enjoy the bites from the bugs that come with the warmer months. Yes, you can invest in a laser-guided, space-age fly swatter, but mosquitoes and other nigh-on invisible biters will get you in the end. Here's what to do.

When a mosquito bites, it injects proteins under our skin to prevent our blood from clotting – our skin reacts to the proteins and this is what causes the intense itching. But listen up: heat destroys these proteins. So one way to relieve the itchiness is to apply a heated spoon to the bite for a couple of minutes (warm the spoon under a hot tap for a minute but be careful not to scald yourself). It's either that, spending a fortune on something from the pharmacy or wrapping yourself in cling film.

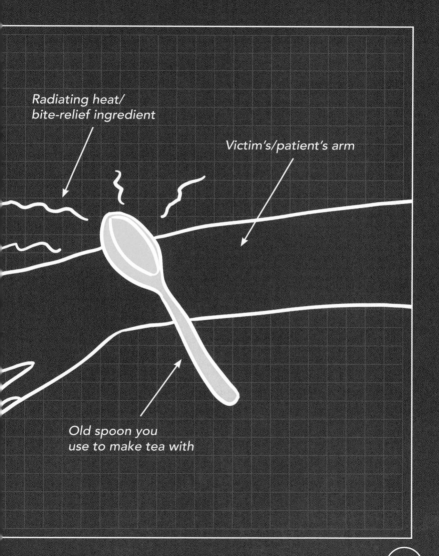

Radiating heat/
bite-relief ingredient

Victim's/patient's arm

Old spoon you
use to make tea with

SEEING IN THE DARK

Here's a shot in the dark (get it?!). Seriously, though, this hack might not get used too often (there's a thing called a torch, you know), but when you're caught short, it could be very handy.

The next time you go camping (or you're staying at a friend's house and can't find the light switch), try using this trick to improve your night vision. Focus your gaze just off-centre of the direction you are moving in. By using your peripheral vision, you'll engage more photoreceptors (or 'rods') at the back wall of the eye, which help you to identify shapes and movement in low light. Forget the lies about eating carrots and try this for size.

Shifty, side-glancing eyes

Completely useless light source

TEABAG BOOT DEODORISER

Strolling in the countryside is all kinds of fun, but if you're unlucky enough to suffer from serious bouts of 'stinkfoot', you might want to do yourself and your family a favour by following this advice.

By placing a fresh teabag in your boots or trainers overnight, you'll help to keep any bad odours at bay. Just don't confuse the de-stinker with a drinker – otherwise you'll be left with a bad taste in your mouth too.

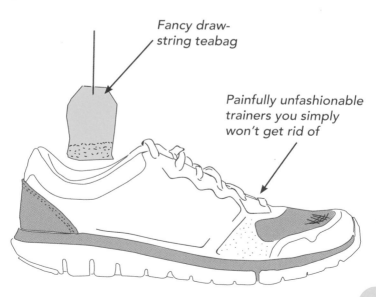

Fancy draw-string teabag

Painfully unfashionable trainers you simply won't get rid of

BACKPACK BIN LINER

If you insist on dragging your beloved family around the woods while you live out your Bear Grylls fantasy, you need to be prepared. One thing your kids won't stand for is soggy sandwiches – so ensure that everything in your backpack is perfectly dry with this simple hack.

Use a thick bin bag to line the inside of your bag. Sure, it won't last as long as a professional liner, but it will cost considerably less.

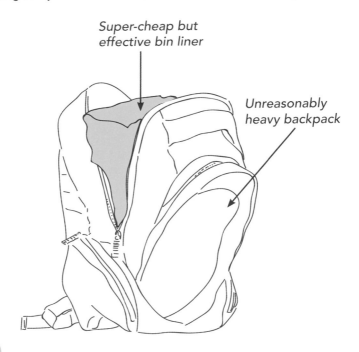

Super-cheap but effective bin liner

Unreasonably heavy backpack

CLOTHING AND GROOMING HACKS

Dads have their own unique sense of style – maybe you've rocked the socks-and-sandals combo or sported the occasional Hawaiian shirt yourself? If so, you need help. Even those of you who think you know a thing or two about style will find something here to raise your game. Just don't spoil it by breaking out into your goofiest 'dad dance' at the next wedding party. No amount of sharp tailoring can cover up that embarrassment.

COLLAR STRAIGHTENERS

Have you ever put on a shirt only to discover that the collar has creases in it? Don't waste precious minutes by breaking out the ironing board – fix it the *Life Hacks* way!

Grab some hair straighteners (don't bother asking your wife beforehand, as she will only say no!), turn them on, allow them to reach full temperature and then proceed to use them as a mini-iron by clasping your collar ends and 'straightening' them out. And be careful: hot straighteners + bare skin = bad times.

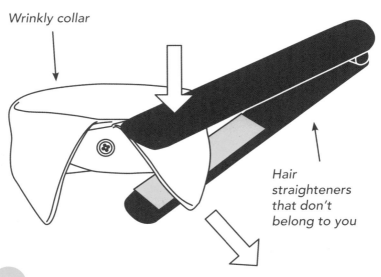

Wrinkly collar

Hair straighteners that don't belong to you

STUCK ZIPPER RELEASE

A zipper is a pretty simple bit of technology – it goes up and it goes down. At least that's how it should work. But somehow this most basic of sartorial exercises can go wrong, and you can end up flying your flag at half-mast, if you know what I mean.

Don't sweat it. If you rub a graphite pencil (the pointy end) over the zipper teeth, you should be able to unzip the zip. Vaseline, lip balm and crayons can work too. Just be careful if you're working in the trouser area – especially if you've just sharpened your pencil.

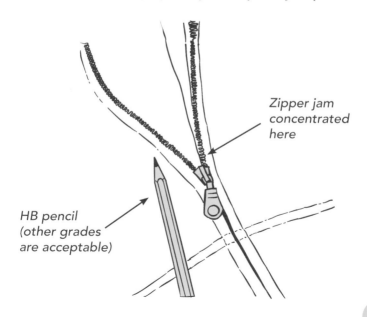

Zipper jam
concentrated
here

HB pencil
(other grades
are acceptable)

LEMON SWEAT-STAIN REMOVER

We've all seen those deodorant ads where the good-looking guy swans around all sweat-free and confident. Reality is far smellier and soggier. So how do you remove a stubborn sweat or deodorant stain from your favourite T-shirt?

Scrub the area with a mix of equal parts water and lemon juice, and then hang your garment out to dry in the sun (I believe the technical term for this is 'sun bleaching'). No sun? Just throw your lemony T-shirt in the wash. Take that, implausible deodorant guy!

Manual citric acid extraction pincer unit

Lemon wedge expressing tangy liquid contents

IRON-FREE IRONING

We've already dealt with de-creasing your shirt collar (see p.130) – so let's look at the rest. If you haven't got the time or the energy to iron your shirt, hang it in the bathroom whilst you're having a shower and see how the wrinkles will disappear. For maximum effect, close your bathroom window and door, get your shirt as close to the water as you can without it getting wet, and have a hot shower for a good 10 or 15 minutes.

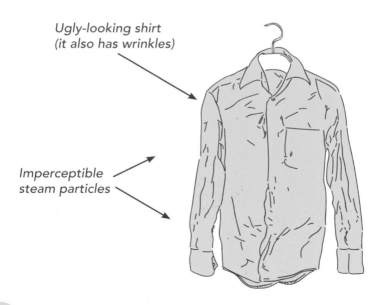

*Ugly-looking shirt
(it also has wrinkles)*

*Imperceptible
steam particles*

FREEZER JEAN CLEAN

If you thought showering with your shirt was weird, this hack will freak you out. Men often have numerous pairs of jeans – maybe some for painting in, some for relaxing in and some for 'best'. Well, to keep your 'best' jeans looking 'best' you want to avoid over-washing, which causes the denim to fade. If you can get over how odd this sounds, here's how you can keep your jeans pristine.

Fold them into a plastic bag and place them in the freezer for 24 hours to kill off any bacteria. Just remember that this isn't a substitute for washing when the jeans are stained – that gross glob of curry will just get harder when frozen.

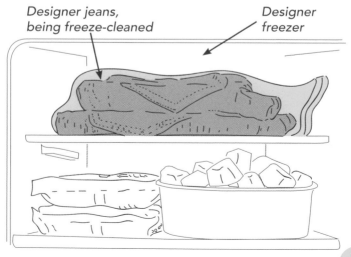

Designer jeans, being freeze-cleaned

Designer freezer

CLOSET CLEAR-OUT

We've shown you how to expand your wardrobe's holding capacity space, now here's a way to make more room.

Once a year, reverse the hangers so that your clothes are hanging backwards. After you've worn an item, put it back in the wardrobe with the hanger the right way round again. After a few months you'll easily be able to see which clothes you never touch and so would make ideal donations for charity shops. Remember to be brutal – do you really need the beer-stained Superman onesie you wore on your stag do?

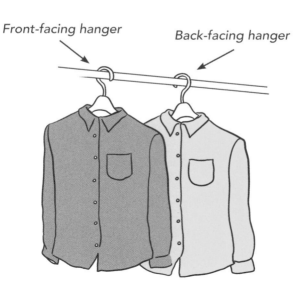

Front-facing hanger

Back-facing hanger

RESTRING A DRAWSTRING

If you've ever lost the drawstring to your jogging bottoms or hoodie, you'll know what a pain it is to get the darn thing back in again. How can it be so easy for the string to work its way out, yet impossible to get it back in?

Here's what you need to do: thread the string into a drinking straw and staple it at the far end so that it stays put. Then feed the straw through your hood or waistband until it comes out the other end. Remove the drinking straw and remember to double-knot the string – otherwise, you'll have to do this all over again in the not-too-distant future.

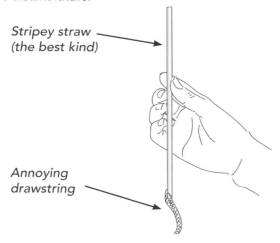

Stripey straw (the best kind)

Annoying drawstring

WORK SHIRT SHUTTLE

This is one for all you cycling commuter dads. If you have the energy and the inclination to cycle to work (as if running around after your adorable children wasn't enough), chances are you're going to change once you arrive at the office. If you have a job where a freshly pressed shirt is a must, take this little piece of advice.

Cut out a piece of thick cardboard (an old box will do) to the size of an A4 piece of paper. Reinforce it packing tape – a few times along the length and the same along the width, and at the edges. You now have a sturdy board to fold your shirt around. Place your shirt front-side down on a flat surface and place the board on top of it, so the top (shorter) edge of the board is level with the bottom of your collar. Fold your sleeves into the middle of the board and then position them running down its length. Next, fold the bottom portion of your shirt up onto the board – you should end up with a shirt that's packed like it is on the shelf in the store. To finish, simply slip the shirt-board combo into a plastic bag and voila – your waterproof, anti-crease shirt transportation system is complete.

A4 piece of card

Strong tape reinforcement

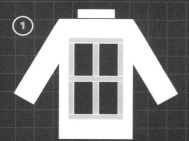

① Place card onto shirt

② Fold in sleeves

(Sleeves folded)

④ Fold up shirt tail

⑤ The finished and boarded shirt

⑥ Slip into a bag

BAG

DIY BEARD OIL

Every man, at some point in his life, is tempted to sport a beard. It's an old-school dad look that says you're a confident, capable, hands-on kind of guy. Like maybe you could take out a bear with your fists. But to keep your face fuzz looking good, you need to give it some grooming attention.

Beard oil will combat itching and keep you looking smooth. Forget paying through the nose for it, though – make your own. Take a small bottle of carrier oil (e.g. sweet almond or coconut oil) and add a few drops of essential oil, such as cedarwood, lemongrass or peppermint. These oils are strong, so be careful: only add a few drops. Then shake the bottle and massage a few drops into your whiskers for beardy bliss.

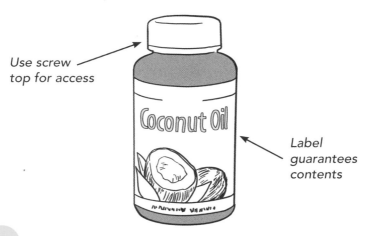

Use screw top for access

Coconut Oil

Label guarantees contents

SUIT JACKET BUTTONS

Whether you enjoy dressing in a suit or not, chances are you want to look good when you do. To avoid looking like a turkey in your Sunday best, follow these rules for buttons on a single-breasted jacket.

One-button jackets: button when standing, unbutton when sitting. Two-button jackets: button the top, never the bottom (same rule applies for standing and sitting). For three-button jackets: button the middle and never the bottom – the top button is optional. Don't forget it!

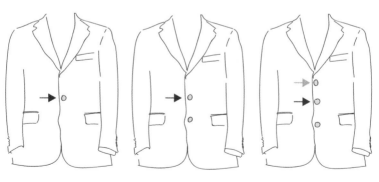

One-button suit   *Two-button suit*   *Three-button suit*

SHAVING RAZOR SAVER

If you're the kind of guy that enjoys the silky smooth satisfaction of a wet shave, this hack is for you – especially if you're inclined to splash out on those fancy multi-blade razors.

One of the most annoying things about wet-shaving – aside from ending up covered in red spots and little pieces of toilet paper (if this happens to you on a regular basis, for god's sake give up) – is the fact that decent razors cost so much these days. Save yourself a packet by extending the life of your existing razors: after each use, blast the blade(s) with a hairdryer. This will eliminate residual moisture and so help prevent oxidization and dulling.

That should keep your face and your wallet happy – at least until you get tempted to buy the new even-more-effective-because-it-has-yet-another-blade razor.

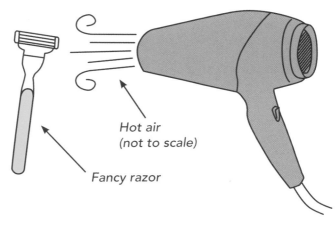

*Hot air
(not to scale)*

Fancy razor

RANDOM HACKS

To finish off, here's a selection of random hacks – some of them are out-there, while others might just be crazy enough to be useful. You never know… A day might come when you really do have to commit the ultimate 'dadly sin' and set fire to your beloved nacho chips.

WAKE-UP CALL

Don't you hate it when you wake up before your alarm goes off? It's part of being a dad, of course, but once the kids are old enough to know that sleeping in is something to be desired, every extra minute in the caress of that blissful duvet counts.

But did you know that waking up naturally, before your alarm (unless you're interrupted by your cat sitting on your face or by your kids jumping all over you), is actually better for you? So next time you beat the buzzer, do yourself a favour and spring out of bed.

Even your hair will appreciate your early rising

BABY DUST-BUSTER

No doubt you love your little bundle (or bundles) of joy, but what have they done for you lately? If the answer is 'not much' then consider using this next hack.*

If your kid is fond of crawling and wriggling around on the floor like a scamp, why not put those tiny wriggling limbs to work by kitting him or her out with a mop-frilled onesie. They can be put together easily by cutting up one of those car 'hand mops' and sewing it to the arms and legs of the onesie. Voila! You have yourself a dust-busting, clean-as-you-wriggle baby!

*Please note: if you care even remotely about your baby, please do not use this hack.

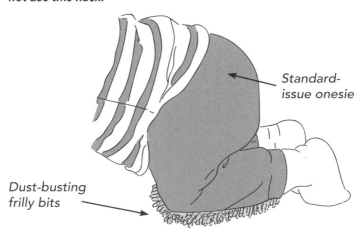

Standard-issue onesie

Dust-busting frilly bits

RE-PING YOUR PONG

Who wants a game of ping-pong?! Well, you can't – the ball is dented. It wasn't me, honest! Removing the dents is actually pretty easy. Hold a lighter underneath the ball (not too close, though) and the gases inside the ball will heat up and expand, forcing the ball back into its original shape.

If you don't have access to a lighter, putting the ball into a boiling pan of water will have the same effect. Just be careful when removing it; boiling water can be a little 'burny'.

Dented ping-pong ball

Lighter

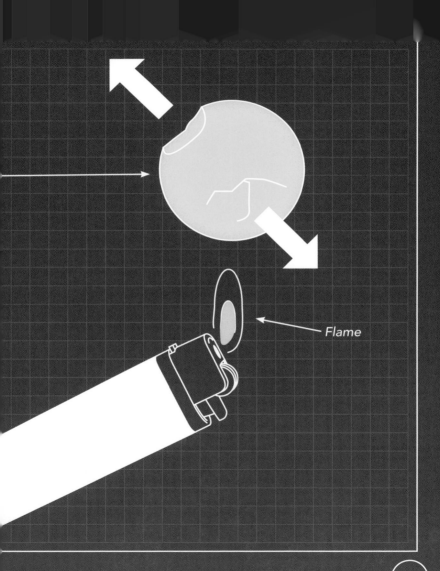

Flame

TORTILLA CHIP KINDLING

The wilderness called and you answered. Your survival instincts so far have been great. You've built a shelter and caught some food. Well done, but how are you going to start the campfire without any kindling?

It's lucky that you remembered the tortilla chips. No, you're not going to eat them. Tortilla chips actually make great kindling. Pile them up and set them alight – you'll be eating in no time. Just not tortilla chips!

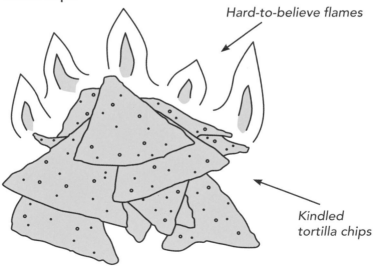

Hard-to-believe flames

Kindled tortilla chips

SNOW SKID PADS

So you've been a complete idiot and gone out driving in the snow. You might have really wanted that bumper pack of red rope licorice, but you're paying the price now – you're bumper-deep in white stuff and your tyres are squealing like a crazed robot pig. You need some assistance.

Before you give in and call recovery, try this little hack on for size: remove the mats from your footwell and wedge them in tight in front of your tyres (front or rear depends on whether your car is front- or rear-drive, dummy). The mats will provide much needed grip and could potentially get you out of your slippery situation.

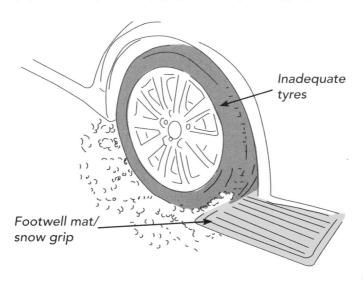

Inadequate tyres

Footwell mat/ snow grip

LIFE OF PI

No, this isn't about how to survive an amazing journey on a boat with a tiger. This is about the value pi. Maybe you can remember learning about this mathematical marvel back in school – and you probably said: 'When the hell am I going to use this again?' Well, you'd be surprised how useful it can be. Like when you want to impress your friends by recalling the first eight numbers by heart.

Simply commit the phrase: 'May I have a large container of coffee' to memory. The numerical values of pi relate directly to how many letters are in each word of the phrase, i.e. 'May' is 3, 'I' is 1, 'have' is 4, etc. Just remember that 'pi' goes with 'coffee' and you're made.

Pi (not pie)

3.14159265359

There are many more numbers after this, but to remember them you'll need a better hack

NO-MORE-TANGLES HEADPHONES

Modern life is full of little problems – that's what this book is about, after all. But right up there at the top of the list of most annoying ones is headphones tangle. Yes, you can use the little pouch they come in – methodically folding them up and securing them – but you'd better believe that when it comes to unravelling them, you will end up with a wiry mess.

You need a compact spooling system, courtesy of your old tape dispenser. Simply spool your headphones wire onto the tape ring, leaving the jack exposed at the back and the phones nestled at the front. Now you can listen to REO Speedwagon without getting really angry beforehand.

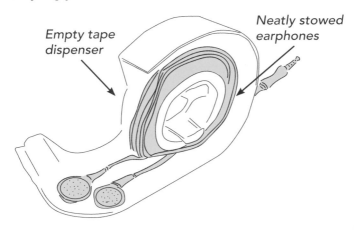

Empty tape dispenser

Neatly stowed earphones

FINAL WORD

Now you have acquired a wealth of Life Hack knowledge, you can consider yourself a better person and – more importantly – a significantly superior dad. You're the king of 'can do' – even if that amounts to you being more efficient at drinking beer and devouring burgers while cracking walnuts with one hand. The wonders of Life Hacks never cease!

HACKS INDEX

COMMANDO DAD
Mission Adventure

Neil Sinclair

£9.99
Paperback
ISBN: 978-1-84953-884-8

Rally the troops – It's time for adventure.

Ex-commando and dad of three Neil Sinclair follows his bestselling parenting manual *Commando Dad: Basic Training* with this guide bursting with ideas for getting active with your kids.

This fully illustrated field manual is packed with dozens of missions for you and your troops to enjoy, including:

- creative projects in Base Camp
- outdoor missions at home and away
- activities for mobile and junior troopers

All with expert advice and carefully drafted mission briefs to make sure you get the most out of your time together.

Discover the tried-and-tested Commando Dad approach to parenting and teach your young troopers to be the best they can be!

GET YOUR

SH!T

TOGETHER

**HOW TO CHANGE YOUR LIFE
BY TIDYING UP YOUR STUFF
& SORTING OUT YOUR HEAD SPACE**

VICKI VRINT

GET YOUR SH!T TOGETHER
How to Change Your Life By Tidying Up Your Stuff & Sorting Out Your Head Space

Vicki Vrint

£6.99

Hardback

ISBN: 978-1-84953-794-0

Organise your stuff and organise your life – you'll soon see the results.

This book tells you *exactly* how to get your sh*t together, so you can be the best version of yourself. Use its winning blend of super-achievable life hacks, motivating quotations and lots of good sh*t to kick-start your transformation.

If you're interested in finding out more about
our books, find us on Facebook at
Summersdale Publishers
and follow us on Twitter at
@Summersdale

WWW.SUMMERSDALE.COM

IMAGE CREDITS